Hope Rising

A JOURNEY OF
FAITH, HOPE, & HEALING

By
Misty Bacon

Hope Rising
A Journey of Faith, Hope, and Healing
© 2022 by Misty Bacon

Printed in the United States of America.
ISBN-13: 978-1-7372768-9-0
LCCN: 2022901055

Misty's Books
Pasadena, TX

TABLE OF CONTENTS

INTRODUCTION

I am successful entrepreneur devoted to living a pure lifestyle despite being tempted by lust and the desire for true love, finding it more difficult to honor my vow to the Lord, which I have tried to renegotiate a thousand times. God has reminded me to quit *"throwing your pearls to swine."* I desperately want to honor my commitment to the Lord but also yearn for companionship.

Will I deviate from my commitment to the Lord, a vow I made after my divorce to stay pure until my wedding night, staying the course to receive God's best for my life? A beautiful, amazing relationship that will bless, honor, support, and protect me for the rest of my life, or will I derail that path to temporarily satisfy my flesh?

The purpose of this book is to share how my life has been with Christian dating in a Snapchat, Facebook Live, Instagram Reels, and TikTok world. I am a forty-something single Christian living in a time where almost the entire world is on social media, but there are still people that have not heard the name Jesus or held, much less, read out of a Bible.

The year 2020 was a year of clear and perfect vision. I have struggled to write what I know the Lord has asked of me. Last year was filled with revelation, cleansing, and discovery; however, with that comes pain and frustration.

I have often struggled with direction and being stunned by fear. Why do we get stunned or frozen with fear? We let it paralyze us. I know the Word of God is true, living, and have seen it lived out right in front of my eyes many times. So why did I let fear paralyze me to what I know was God speaking to me? I will say this, the Lord reveals himself when one's heart and mind are open.

I hope this book encourages you to be honest with yourself, take an inventory of things you need to let go of, and learn you can live a life free from guilt, fear, and anxiety. You are strong, courageous, and deserve to live life to the fullest. You are not alone. You have a purpose, and God's not done with you yet!

"Visions, hopes, and dreams
sometimes melt away
like ice cream, they fade,
dripping on a hot summer day.
People, time, and life can get in
the way,
stealing those precious gifts that
were meant to stay."
-Misty Bacon

THE "M" IN MISTY

"I always wanted, and still aspire, to be something more than just one thing, just one performance."
– Kevin Bacon

MY LIFE AS A BACON

I was born in the seventies and grew up in the awesome eighties when everything was neon, sparkly, side ponytail in a scrunchy, loud boom boxes, Nintendo, and payphones! My ten-year-old nephew once asked my brother on a vacation in Europe, *"Uh, Dad, what's that big box over there?"* Oh, you younger gens have missed so much awesomeness. Life was so much simpler and safe. I guess that is our perception when we are young anyway. Oh, for the record, I am not related to Kevin, although in elementary school, I told everyone we were cousins.

I have lived a super blessed life, even when I did not serve the Lord. I got a job in New York at

3

twenty-two and lived there for four awesome years. I went to opening day of Wimbledon, ate Indian food in London for the first time, flew first class, and had filet minion—that was the best filet I have ever had to this day. While in New York, I lived in Brooklyn and rode the subway to work every day. And I started standup comedy. Who gets to travel the world in first class at twenty-two years old? **This girl,** and with braces on. What! I got braces my senior year in college, thank you, Aunt Sandy!

I made so many wonderful friends in New York. New York was beyond awesome, like tubular, totally rad. The company I worked for merged with another, and I talked them into giving me a package so I could move to Los Angeles, which was a childhood dream since I was two years old.

Los Angeles was short-lived, but it was fun. I lived with my aunt and uncle at first, but then got a studio apartment, where I experienced my first and last earthquake.

My uncle was a personal trainer to the stars, so meeting them was commonplace. My first Thanksgiving was with Diane Lane and her daughter. One afternoon, I came home to hear Johnny Fever's voice in the kitchen. Yes! It was Howard Hessman in the kitchen talking to my aunt. Howard played a DJ on WKRP in Cincinnati. I also met Brad Garret (the brother on *Everybody Loves Raymond*) and George Lopez (*The George Lopez Show*) at the Ice House in Pasadena, where I was a hostess and performed on the side, a much smaller stage. That is where all the up-and-coming comedians performed. I also met Loni Love (@therealdaytime and regular on World's Dumbest Criminals) and in New York with Jim Gaffigan (if you don't know who he is, Google him. **Oh my lanta**, he is funny).

I was never a big dater. I had one boyfriend most of high school and part of my freshman year in college, another one in college, and that's about it. Well, I met a boy on classmates.com or Myspace . . . What! Is that even still around . . . it could be. Who knows? We went to high school together, but I don't remember him . . . shh, don't tell him. We dated on and off before I met Mr. Right, well, Mr. Right then.

I prayed to meet someone I could love as I had never loved before and for him to love as he had never loved before. When I met **him**, I stopped praying. I had just moved back from Los Angeles, living with my cousin and some of her teacher friends in a rent house. I went to my parents' house for Fourth of July, and I walked over to their neighbors' house, who were having a party, a BBQ; that is how we do things in the South.

This handsome, blue-eyed, super muscular guy walked over, put his hand out, and said, "My name is"—let us call him Sam. I said, "I've heard a lot about you, and most of it was not nice." Can you believe I said that? I did. It should have been a sign, right? We ended up going to watch fireworks, and the rest is history.

We had a very passionate relationship. We did everything together, working out, grocery shopping, and we watched a lot of TV. We got engaged after dating for nine months and moved in together after a year. We got married at the justice of the peace, after knowing each other for two years because he had a son, and in the divorce decree, no person of the opposite sex could stay after 10 pm at night.

I was **not** a bridezilla. Actually, I told Mom, "No matter what happens, only you and I know how everything is supposed to be." So, there was no getting upset. Well, the morning started with this truth, I did not like the way the cosmetologist fixed my hair. And that is a **big** deal, right? I did my own makeup and ended up getting mascara on my dress, not once, not twice but actually **three** times. I did not put makeup on while **in** my dress. I may be blond, but I'm not ridiculous.

I did not have something borrowed, so my amazing aunt, same one who paid for my braces, let me wear her gold bracelet. I am not fond of gold; I'm more of a platinum girl. However, I was grateful.

A dear friend from New York came down, and when we arrived at the church, my mom held the side door open with this look of frustration. "The flowers . . ." she scowled. Oh no, what in the world could it be? I thought they were beautiful, however they were not what we had ordered. Let's just say whoever got mine would not have been happy at all. I had chosen a bunch of purple flowers, and the ones I got had a lot of roses . . . Eek, I feel sorry for whoever had to answer the call at the flower shop that day.

Side Note:

Before the ceremony, my husband took a shot because he was nervous and decided to call me to tell me that he had taken a shot. I was furious, mostly because I was already in my dress, and no one would let me eat or drink. But I said, "Do you not want to get married?" He said, "Of course, I want to marry you, but I am nervous to be in front of all those people and mostly because of your dad." My dad did **not** like him, and that's an understatement.

To this day, if anyone says his name, he has a very bad reaction.

One of my bridesmaids did not get to make it. She was supposed to take a train from Los Angeles to Houston, but Amtrak had a derailment; therefore, she could not attend.

One of the groomsmen went to jail and also could not attend. At the reception, **he** got drunk and had everyone do keg stands, even my poor grandmother. Real classy. Oh, and our unity candle, which my mom's cousin had made, didn't light. Ya think there were warning signs?

As I mentioned before, we had a very passionate relationship, but it was superficial. He liked to push my buttons to provoke me. In his defense, I didn't open up to him about my emotions from my past. I experienced depression and was diagnosed as bipolar while we were engaged, and I was even on medication. However, I decided to stop taking them as I was tired of feeling like a zombie. He also encouraged me to go to therapy, which I did, and started standing up to him, to which he decided I no longer needed therapy.

After four years of this fight, then make-up, he decided he didn't want to be married anymore. He loved me; he was just not **in love** with me.

So, I married in 2007 for four years and then divorced at age thirty-three, the same age Jesus was when he died. Ironically, I died that year as well. I had the most beautiful encounter with the Lord. I was boohooing; I mean snot bubbles, hiccups, and sobbing while rocking in my family's rocking chair, a chair my brother and I used to fight over who got it. I am the oldest grandchild on the Bacon side, I should get it, right? Ah no, my brother, the only boy on the Bacon side, thought he should get it. He did get it for a couple years as he was the first to have children. Now my dad has it, which means, I will get it!

I'm Daddy's girl, and my brother knows it. My brother is my mom's favorite because he gave her grandchildren. I told him the second I get pregnant, he drops status, which we both laugh at, mostly because I'm forty-five, not dating, and perimenopausal.

I totally forgot where I was going with this . . . oh, sobbing while going through a divorce. So, if you don't know what it's like, let me share. It feels like your insides are ripping and now exposed on the outside of your body. The Bible does say the two become one flesh, which means you are literally ripping that apart. "Ouch," as E. T. would say.

Back to my story: I was weeping and saying, "Lord, I don't want to live like this; it hurts toooo much"; yes, you need that many oooos to truly understand the pain. I said, "Lord, if you don't show me how to live, I don't want to live anymore. Show me how to live life, truly live life." And, then I fell to my knees. I felt a warmth come over me like a blanket that comforted me. At that moment, I knew I was in the arms of my Father, the only one who could rescue me.

He rescued me from depression, being molested in elementary school, and being cheated on by boyfriends and ultimately my husband. In that moment, I knew my life was changed. I knew I was saved by His grace that he freely gave on the cross some 2000 years ago. The scripture in 2 Corinthians 5:17 says, "Therefore, if anyone is in Christ, the new creation has come; thus, old has gone, the new is here!" That was February 2007. I changed back to my maiden name in September and then vowed to the Lord I would not have sex until my wedding night.

Wait . . .

What just happened?!

"Lord, did I really say that? What I meant was . . ."

OK.

"Fine, Lord, I mean . . .

"I will stay pure until my wedding night!

"I am now yours!"

II

THE "I" IN MISTY

"I will submit and allow for unconditional love from and to others, giving me freedom and others the opportunity to be close to me, to be vulnerable, exposed and not in control."
– John Bevere in his book *The Bait of Satan*

I'M WAITING

In 2008, a friend of mine thought it was a good idea for me to start dating. I was like, oh no, I am not ready, not ready at all! Reluctantly, I got on Christian Mingle, eHarmony, and I think Match.com. It is sad and funny that I can't remember. Anywho, I went on several dates, but I was not ready. Most men just wanted a hook-up, and I wasn't remotely interested, and that I had vowed to God Almighty that I would stay pure.

I did meet a guy on one of the above mentioned; he was tall, handsome, and muscular. We texted and talked on the phone a little, and he finally asked me out to a nice dinner at a place that had a live jazz band. He was classy; that was a good start.

We ordered food, and then he said, "So, I'm divorced; I don't want to get married again. I have two kids; I do not want any more children, and I was raised Pentecostal, but now I'm atheist. How about you?" I felt I was in *The Twilight Zone*. I said, "Well, I, too, am divorced and definitely want to get married again. I do not have children but would love the opportunity to have them, and I am totally into Jesus." We ended up having a really good time.

That night, he texted that he had such a great time, blah blah blah. I said, "I had a good time as well." He texted that he would like to go out again. **Really**? I said, "No, thank you. We want different things. We should just walk away now so no one gets their feelings hurt." He asked, "Why?" **Really**? I said, "Well, first of all, I want to get married, have children, and a relationship with the Lord." **Hello**! "You do not want to get married AGAIN, have more children, and don't believe in God. So why would we even consider?" He said, "Well, I could consider getting married again and kids." I said, "STOP right there. You meant what you said last night. And I'm not interested in being with someone who doesn't have the same goals, AND you shouldn't have to settle." He replied, "NO, we have so much in common. I can come around." Can you believe this guy? I said, "No, I think we are done! Good luck dating, and I hope you find someone."

A couple of years went by, and I was in beast mode. I got my real estate license, went on awesome vacations, mission trips, and to church any time the doors were open. A pastor friend of mine said I needed to be at the church anytime the doors were open. And I definitely recommend it as the best way to heal and be discipled. I went to prayer on Tuesday nights, church on Wednesdays and Sundays, and the ladies Bible study once a month.

I also started going to other churches to see if there were other singles my age. Most people in church were married or way older or way younger. Where in the world were people my age?

Another friend created a profile and started swiping for me on OkCupid, another dating site. I think I might need new friends. Just kidding. I actually have amazing friends that are always looking out for me.

The first guy we messaged in the app, messaged for a couple of days and then started texting. He asked if he could call, and I said, "Give me an hour." On the hour on the **dot**, he texted, "Are you free?" I said, "Give me a few more, finishing up some work." I finally texted that I was free. He immediately called. We chatted for forty-five minutes; well, he **talked** the entire forty-five minutes. He was a teddy bear and a great communicator. Blah blah blah. "I need to stop you right there! I have an early day tomorrow, and, to be honest, I'm not interested . . ."

What I actually said was, "I hate to interrupt, but I have an early and long day tomorrow. It's my grandmother's birthday, and then my dad's the next day, and I'm in charge of planning for both," thinking he would get the hint of a busy day and not able to text a lot. Men are not that smart. When we get off the phone, I brushed my teeth and came back to a text saying he enjoyed our convo, no big deal.

The next morning, he sent two texts. I didn't respond till the afternoon. "Hey, great day, hanging with my grandmother today . . ." He texted two more times in the afternoon, and I did not respond. The next day, I received a message on the app, not via text, "I guess you're not interested." Dude, I told you I was going to be busy! I sent a message back that I was sorry I was not going to meet his expectations of communication, and we would not be a fit.

The second guy said, "Hey, let us do lunch?!" "Ok, here is my number. Text me.

What kind of food?" Dates we are available? Yadda yadda. "Ok, let us have lunch on Friday." "Great."

That Thursday morning, he text, "Hey, looking forward to meeting you tomorrow." Me: "Me too."

Him: "I do not remember if we discussed this or not, but I am in an open marriage." I threw my phone across the room. Are you kidding me? They have websites for you people?

An hour later, I text back, "We did NOT discuss this. Thank you for letting me know. I am going to pass; I wish you the best of luck." He text back: "I understand, but it is only lunch; what is the harm?" I text back: "I DECLINE." He said I was the girl of his dreams in high school, and he would not stop pursuing me. And we were done! I was so done with dating!

Dating was not going well for me! I had changed, technology had changed, and Jiminy Christmas dating had changed. You could no longer just be friends with someone of the opposite sex; either they wanted a friend with benefits, or they wanted to be exclusive. I do not even know if I'm attracted to you; we haven't met! Because you probably do **not** look like your profile picture. And texting every day is not dating. If we do not see each other at least **once** a week, we are not dating!

Yet another friend adamantly said, "You need to be on Bumble." Here we go again. Am I ready this time? My profile said: "I am a hardworking, fun, friendly girl next door. I travel often, volunteer in my community and my profession. Faithfully serves the Lord, helps the homeless, widows and orphans. Mother of one furry baby, she is fifteen years old and my partner in crime. Standup comic in my twenties'. I Love to have fun!"

Chatting with lots of guys can be fun; however, it is more exhausting; an ego boost, but very fleshy. One guy finally asked me out, we went to dinner and then to listen to eighties music. There were lots of high-fives at dinner as we had a lot in common. He was cute, polite, funny, talkative, and a good listener. Then we walked over to Numbers, a dance club, and it was 80s Grunge Night. He asked if I was having fun. Of course, I was. He leaned in and kissed me. Sadly, I felt nothing. I could feel his touch but no chemistry, or was it God protecting me? Oh yes, this was Wedneday night before Thanksgiving. I was getting up at five o'clock am the next day to drive to Fredericksburg with my family.

We said we would talk after Thanksgiving. He text Friday or Saturday to see how Turkey Day went. Then on late afternoon Sunday, he said, "Are you home yet?" "No, in route now." We chit-chatted about Christmas decorations, and I think I said, "Please tell me you are wearing PJs and watching Christmas movies on Hallmark." He made a tacky reference, and I said, "No, my pastor brags about PJs and watching Christmas movies all the time." He said, "Are you a Bible thumper?" I said, "I do not know how to respond to that." He said, "Then you are." He said, "Do you go to church every Sunday?" I said, "No I go, Saturday nights." He thought I was joking. He said something about sex, and I said, "I would not have slept with you that night anyway." He said, "Then I'm not the guy for you; you should be on eHarmony not Bumble." It stung for a second or two, then I thought, *Lord, this is only a fraction of the persecution you felt.*

I could deal with it. My ego was bruised and my pride was pierced, for sure. "But, Lord, thank you for helping me dodge a bullet." You would think I would learn my lesson, but I did not.

Two days later, I was back on Bumble but happened to be in Memphis with my brother. I met two Memphis men. One was so fun, nice, and polite. Here is the story of the second one. We exchanged numbers and texted for a couple of days. Then on a Friday, he said, "Tell me about your walk with the Lord." I text back, "Would love to but am driving right now." He called, and we talked for forty-five minutes to an hour. At the end of the call, he said, "No matter what happens, know the Lord is in this. Or the Lord has orchestrated it." "I totally agree with you." I really liked his voice. It had a little twang with a little raspy and a lot of the Deep South.

We talked a couple of more times and then came the big wamba jamba conversation I like to call Testimony Tuesday or Freedom Fest . . . He said, "I feel like the Lord wants you to have freedom in an area of your life and that you need to talk about it. You do not have to talk to me but at least talk to someone." Tears streamed down my face.

Have you ever had deep pain in your chest, and it was so heavy and strong? I could barely breathe. I said yes, but I needed to take pictures of a property. "Can I call you back in two minutes?"

A few minutes later, I called him back. Ring, ring, ring. No answer. I did not leave a message. I decided to turn on my radio. A pastor was talking, and he said, ". . . you have been running from the Lord. You want and have asked for freedom in some areas of your life, and now is that time. You can have it today." I boohoo sobbed and snot bubbles cried for who knows however long.

Finally, he called back, and I told him what the pastor said. He said, "Just start talking." I said, "How far back do you want me to go?" He said, "As far back as you want to go." So, I said, "In the beginning was the Word, and the Word was . . ." He said, "You are stalling." I was stalling! Joking was my defense mechanism; we all have one. Joking or changing the subject is mine; avoidance—that is the safe way to protect yourself.

I put both of my hands on my face, and I saw two roads. I could choose the road I always took, with jokes, side-stepping my hurts and pain, or I could Robert Frost it and take the road less traveled upon, that I had **never** taken, to tell a stranger things I had never told anyone.

Ok, here it goes: I was molested as a child, cheated on by my first love in high school, and my first sexual encounter was not technically rape but was not ideal. My husband cheated on me. I was not able to get pregnant, had endometriosis in the past, and several surgeries with the last one taking my right ovary. I drank **a lot** in college and my early twenties and used sex as a weapon, a way to get back, or to be in control. Oh yeah, and I haven't had

25

sex since 2007 when my husband left me. **Boom**, mic drop!

All during the conversation or what felt like me vomiting on this poor guy who was probably rethinking his swipe right, he was so encouraging, sympathetic, such a great listener, and said all the right things at the right time. He said, "I want you to know the Lord showed me two things before you started talking. One, that you were molested, and two, that you were celibate." It is just like the Lord to bring a man to help you/me get through some major hurts that were caused by men." Well, **yes**! It is just like God to bring a man to help a hurt lady who thought she was over the past, had forgiven the molester, her ex-husband, God, and herself.

The next month and a half were filled with deep conversations about God, life, love, business, eighties songs and movies, sending each other YouTube videos of love songs, Queen, Huey Lewis & The News, and, of course, Scripture. Toward the end, it started getting weird.

We had major differences in our beliefs, which were a huge deal breaker for me. It regarded submission and what that looked like. We both agreed it was biblical, but we did not agree what that looked like practically in our own lives.

Over the course of a couple of months of talking, he would use the word *submit* or *submission*. The third time he said it, it was like a time bomb went off inside of me and "WHAT YOU TALKING ABOUT, WILLIS?" came out of me. I asked "Ah, what does submission look like to you? Because you have used it several times now" (ok, it had only been three, but I literally have never heard that word by one person so many times, especially when dating. Not even my ex-husband used that word). He said, "Misty, the Bible says . . ." I said, "Stop right there. I KNOW what the Bible says about submission. I want to know what you think submission looks like and especially in a relationship with you." And that's when Memphis man became a turkey. He wanted a woman to be on the sidelines cheering him on and doing whatever he said, no questions asked; no if, ands, or buts. "You do what I say, I am the man!" "Me Tarzan, you Jane!"

"Well, I am definitely not the girl for you. I am on the field, cheering with my husband! I am not a sideline kinda girl." **Boom**! Mic drop!

I am sorry, not sorry, but I cannot watch someone heading for a head-on collision and not say anything. That was my analogy to him when we called it off. I said, "If we were in a car, and you are driving, I cannot warn you that a car is heading straight for us, AND if I did that, you would choose to stay the course because you are not going to be told what to do by a woman. Just so you know, I'm the kind of WOMAN that will take any and all passengers, and we are jumping out before the collision." And I jumped off the crazy train before a serious collision.

I am grateful for being able to share and heal from intimate details of my past and learn more about what I do and **do not** want in my future husband. I told the Lord if that was what godly men were like, I think He should bring me an atheist or agnostic (hahaha). At least I could work with that. Or I could just trust the Lord that He knows better about what I need and has someone amazing for me. And I need to stop trying to pursue it myself. The Bible does state to seek first His kingdom and His righteousness, and all these things will be given to you (Matt. 6:33).

The Lord has been trying to get me to rest, slow down, and chill out for quite some time, probably most of my life, actually. I am not sure if the Lord works on you the same way, but one day, I opened a book I had been reading, *The Deborah Anointing* by Michelle McClain-Walters, to page forty-four, and in **bold** letters, "Keys to Dwelling in the Secret Place." And not a minute later, Phil Wickham's song, "Secret Place" came on. Ya think the Lord is trying to get my attention! Lord, I hear you. I stop, and with a stream of tears, I say, thank you for loving me and never leaving or forsaking me. The scripture listed in Michelle's book, God says in Psalm 91:1, "Whoever dwells in the shelter of the most-high will rest in the shadow of the Almighty. I will say of the Lord, He is my refuge & my fortress, my God in whom I trust."

With a little word search, I learned:

Dwell – verb, to remain, live as a resident, to keep the attention directed

Shelter – verb, place under protection

Rest – noun, sleep, freedom from activity or labor, inactivity, place to lodge, peace of mind or spirit, something used for support, free of anxieties

Rest – verb, to get rest by lying down, to lie dead, to cease from action or motion, to be based or founded, to remain confident

Shadow – noun, partial darkness within a space from which rays from a source of light are cut off by an interposed opaque body, a reflected image, shelter from danger or observation, imitation of something (copy), an inseparable companion or follower, small degree of portion, pervasive and dominant influence

Shadow – verb, shelter, protect, conceal, to accompany and observe

Shadow – adj, having an indistinct pattern

Refuge – noun, shelter or protection from danger or distress

Fortress – noun, fortified place, stronghold

Trust – noun, assured reliance on the character, ability, strength, or truth of someone or something, one in which confidence is placed, dependence on something future or contingent, hope

Real estate – reliance on future payment for property delivered

I remain in the protection of the Most High and will refrain from activity, free from anxieties of this world in the reflected image of the Almighty. I will say of the Lord, he is my protection from danger and distress and my fortified place, stronghold, and God in whom I put my confidence of his character, ability, and strength to take care of and protect me. And I was able to rest in Lord for a little while.

One morning while walking Lady, my pit rottie. Who is awesome by the way, oh and she used to lick my tears while I was going through my divorce. Shortly after the divorce my mom said you should probably get rid of your dogs. I was like, Lady licked my tears, how can you even think that. Anyway while on this particular walk I heard a bird singing, probably calling for its mate. Well it made me cry and laugh at the same time. The sun was just coming up, and I had just finished working out, like at 5 am. It was beautiful, and at that moment, I knew and could feel God's love for me. He loves each of us so very much, no one more than another.

In seasons of waiting, we can become frustrated, annoyed, bitter, depressed, and even jealous as we watch others be blessed or what seems like they are being blessed while we feel like we are being passed by. Waiting is an active word. Google says waiting is the **action** of staying where one is or delaying action until a particular time or until something else happens. It's also an official attendance at court. Priscilla Shier once said, "Waiting is essential to fruitfulness and usefulness." Anyone that has been to court as a complainant or defendant, and especially as a juror knows what it's like to **wait**. Oh, my lanta; it's brutal and excruciating to sit there waiting. Will we be called next? Nope . . . Ok, we will get called up today. Nope. Oh wait, they are rescheduling us in two weeks from now.

However, it's in the waiting we find more juicy info; to use in court. Or in waiting for a mate, we learn more about what we want and what we **don't** want. We learn more about ourselves. We do not realize we were selfish in an area of our lives. "Oh, I've always wanted to volunteer," then **do it now**! Ask God for revelation on what **you** need to work on, not "Oh Lord, hurry up and bring the right one."

If we focus on waiting for the right one, we will miss the **only one** we need to focus on, God! You thought I was going to say **you**, didn't you? Well, when you focus on God and put him first, Scripture says all these things will be given to you as well.

I love The Passion Translation (TPT) of this in Matthew 6:33. "So above all, constantly seek God's kingdom and his righteousness, then all these LESS important things will be given to you abundantly."

Does that mean God doesn't care about us wanting companionship, our career, or that I need to lose forty-five pounds (insert what is important to you). **No**, what He is saying is that if you focus on the **most** important thing, which is a deep, pure relationship with God, then He will give you all the less important things. Because when you focus on Him, **all** other things become less important.

Do you really know God, or do you just know **about** God? Personal knowledge of Christ will change your life. And you can only get that by seeking Him.

What does that look like? I heard a message by Dr. Charles Stanley that really hit me good in the gut. He says, "Spend time with God every day." Find **quiet** time for seven days to listen for what God wants to say to you. His three key points were:

- Commitment
- Self-discipline
- Submission

Commitment means the state or quality of being dedicated to a cause. Are we committing our hearts, minds, and souls to God, which allows him access to heal every part of us and frees our minds from worry, anxiety, and frustration, and gives him permission to mold and refine us to become all we am called to be. **Yes**, we are being called to be Marines for God.

Self-discipline is the ability to control one's feelings and overcome one's weaknesses; the ability to pursue what one thinks is right despite temptations to abandon it. Wow. I could not have said that better. It is interesting that self-control is the last fruit of the Spirit in Galatians. As women, we definitely could use some help with our feelings, whether we vomit them on people (yikes, please do not do that anymore) or we sweep them under the rug that eventually gets rolled up and shoveled into the attic for a decade. Then one day, it comes crashing down through the ceiling from its massive weight, hits us in the head, and we plop to the floor wondering, "Why now?" Ok, a little dramatic, but aren't we like that? It cannot just be me. We all have weaknesses that can be refined if we schedule Him first and start feeding our spirit instead of our flesh.

And last, but not least, is my good ole friend, submission. Google says it means the action or fact of accepting or yielding to a superior force or to the will or authority of another person. Submission is expressed out of respect by the one submitting. It is not forced by the superior force or authoritative person AKA man.

Only in times of seclusion did Jesus, Paul, and John really hear from and seek God. Those are the most intimate times you will encounter the Lord. Of course, worship and reading the Bible are important, but so is just being still and knowing He is **God**, the great I AM.

During those moments are when I have had the greatest cry fests, revelation, life-changing experiences, and experienced the most healing. Not that we cannot experience those things during a church service or a retreat, but we are more apt to allow ourselves to be vulnerable, exposed, and learn we do not need to always be in control.

There is freedom in losing control or, better yet, submitting control to our Creator. Surrendering your problems, habits, frustrations, and hang-ups to God gives him freedom to heal and deliver us from every one of those things. And that, my friend, only happens while you are waiting, waiting on the King of kings and Lord of lords.

During my season of waiting, I made a bucket list. If you do not have one, I suggest you do it **right now**! **Put** the book down, **stop** reading, and make a list. I do not care if it's only **one** thing. Make a bucket list, share with a friend or two, and ask them to help you do everything on the list. What was on my list, you say?

I. Take a painting class;

II. Skydive;

III. Author (write) a book;

IV. Go to Hawaii;

V. Volunteer, help children;

VI. Eat at every Italian restaurant in Houston to try their tiramisu; and

VII. Travel to Italy.

My friend Jules and I went to Italy in 2013, if I remember correctly, with a church group. The trip was called "Following the Life of Paul." I have to say it was pretty stinking awesome. We took a million pictures. We rode donkeys up the hill of Santorini. We cruised through the Greek Islands; Pizza on Mykonos is literally the cheesiest, spiciest, and yummiest pizza I have **ever** had. We heard a sermon at the Bema seat. And we heard our tour guide read the first chapter of Revelation right before we walked through the cave, where John was exiled and received the revelation to write the book of Revelation. Monks guard it, and I have to say it is the most tranquil experience.

Shortly after that trip, Jules and I went to Painting with a Twist in Houston. We both fell in love with painting, so I invited Jules over one night to scrapbook all the pictures we had taken on our trip. I also purchased cheap canvases, paint, and some brushes. It was so much fun. My first painting after the class was of the Colosseum. It is hideous but one of my favorite paintings.

Some of my other faves are sprinkled through this book. Next on the list was skydiving. I finally got to do this. It was my friend's birthday, and he had posted on Facebook, "I want to go skydiving for my birthday, who's with me?" I totally put the hands-up emoji, and he immediately text me, "Are you serious right now?" It is not scary at all. You feel like a feather floating as you watch everything under you get bigger!

Writing a book has been my biggest struggle. I had the pressure of deadlines and orchestrating it myself and finally got with a publisher to assist. I did tons of research, and you know what they say, "the paralysis of analysis." I say just Nike it . . . **Just do it**.

I got to Hawaii twice! I went once in my twenties and once in my thirties. I think I need to go one more time while I'm still in my forties. So, I'll add that **back** to my bucket list.

Next on my list was to volunteer. I met with a friend about her getting into real estate. We chatted about wanting to help children, how we even start, and where we would go. She went to the bathroom at Panera Bread and came back with a flyer from CASA, which is a Court Appointed Child Advocate for children going through CPS, and they needed volunteers. We went to the informational meeting and training. I have had three cases and have been doing it for three years. I did take a break; it is so emotionally investing. And now I am getting certified to foster. One day, I want to adopt, but for now, I will babysit for foster parents.

I have eaten at a lot of Italian restaurants in Houston but not each one **yet**. Tiramisu, here I come.

New bucket list items that sometimes get carried over to the next year is:

I. Learn to crochet/knit;

II. Go to a dude ranch; there is one in Texas. Who is with me?;

III. Write one letter a month to a total stranger. Just go online and pick a state;

IV. Serve at a shelter on Thanksgiving or Christmas. I have served many, many times but not on a holiday;

V. Travel to Israel with Perry Stone; he teaches a lot on Revelation;

VI. Cooking class;

VII. Pottery class; and

VIII. (NEW) Hawaii before February 2024.

I hope you made your list; if you did not, I challenge you **today** and encourage you to share that list with a trusted friend. Make a plan to do some of these things you might do or want to do before you meet **the right one**. Before you can't do them because when you meet the right one these things don't seem to matter as much as they once did.

To get vulnerable, exposed, not in control, and actively spend time with the Lord is to get to know Him and yourself. It's important to be vulnerable and exposed with the Lord, or you will never be able to with a companion. That is the one thing I learned from my divorce. I didn't open up to him. I didn't allow him to see the real Misty, the hurting Misty. It actually pushed him away.

Being vulnerable and exposed is not comfortable, but Tim Tebow once said, "The more you practice being uncomfortable, the more comfortable you will be in times of discomfort." And we know in this world, there will be times of discomfort, so let's seek the Lord in the waiting so we are prepared and ready when we meet **the right one**! So, while you are waiting, I charge you to reflect on some things:

- Make peace with where you are;
- Make peace with God's timing and his way;

- Do not allow yourself to lose peace over the things you cannot control; and

- Make peace with the fact you can't and shouldn't do everything!

I hope you learn from my adversity, the long season of waiting, so you do not have to wait as long as me ... One journal entry I wrote in 2013, I believe, on Sept 30: *"That you would refine me, restore me, deliver me and help me walk with confidence and authority you have given me. Help me trust you and others. Help me live a righteous life that is pleasing to you and help me quit wrestling with you for control of my life. In Jesus name I surrender. Amen."*

III

THE "S" IN MISTY

"Ruth had to forsake the familiar and comfortable to receive God's best for her life."
– Perry Stone

SACRIFICE NOT NECESSARY, JUST SURRENDER!

Didn't we just talk about being uncomfortable? Here is a perfect example of someone walking away from the familiar and what was comfortable so she could experience God's best. Ruth, in the Bible, just lost her husband, and so did her sister-in-law. The brothers died, and the mother-in-law, Naomi, tells the girls to go back to their homeland and be with their families so they can remarry. Orpah kisses Naomi and runs home.

Ruth, on the other hand, did not, and the Bible says in Ruth 1:14, "But Ruth clung to her." Ruth tells Naomi, "Where you go I will go, where you stay I will stay. Your people will be my people and your God my God." Ruth was a Moabite; they did not know God. She literally chose to go with her mother-in-law (MIL) to a foreign place, to be around foreign people, and learn about a foreign God. That is some sacrifice, right.

Throughout the story, Naomi told Ruth where to go. So, she was obedient to her MIL. And in doing so, she met Boaz, who not only took care of and married her but also took in the mother-in-law, and Naomi got to be a grandmother because Ruth was obedient! I want to meet a Boaz; we all should want to meet a Boaz.

On a hellaciously hot day in June 2020, after a couple of days of being weeping, I prayed that I would totally trust and surrender every part of my heart to the Lord. There was still a part of my heart I had not allowed the Lord to touch, much less heal. I was saved, but I had not surrendered **all** of my heart. I told the Lord that I surrendered, but when it came to men, **I got this**! **Yes**, I really said that to the Lord and am still standing. Hahaha.

I was molested by a man, cheated on by my first love, my first sexual encounter was absolutely a nightmare, and was cheated on by my husband that resulted in a baby. Yes, another woman was having a baby with **my** husband. On top of that, I cannot have children. So why in the world would I trust God? He allowed me to be hurt over and over and over again! He allowed me to be taken advantage by all these men, men he created.

So, what does it look like to surrender? Webster's Dictionary says it is to give (something) over to the control or possession of another usually under duress. Hmm, that is interesting. Most of the time, when people get saved, truly saved, they surrender their hearts to Jesus, asking him to come be Lord of their lives. I would like to share more of my salvation encounter now if you would permit me to.

It was one night while on the couch in my condominium while my then-husband sat in a different chair. Sidebar, we had several series we would watch **every** single night of the week. Now, it's binge watching. There was not a label back then. To an extrovert, this is brutal to not hang out with friends or family but to rush home after dinner, working out, or the grocery store, and just plop on the couch! I have never felt so alone as to when I was married and not connected to that person. I have been single for thirteen years now. I **know** what alone feels like. Anyhow, sitting on my couch, I closed my eyes and said, "Lord, I want to feel you again. I want to live life! I'm sick of watching people live their lives."

Three days later, my then-husband said he wanted a divorce. **What**! I distinctly remember saying, "Lord, this is NOT how I expected you to answer me!" Boom! I packed my bags, pillow, and our box fan! Oh yeah, Momma doesn't sleep without her noise! Who's with me?

I had no idea where I would go. So I called a friend and said, "Whatcha doing tonight?" She said,

"What are you doing tonight?" "Well, I think I'm getting a divorce." She said, "Where are you?" "In your driveway," I said. She said, "Come on in." We visited for a little while, and her husband made us something to eat. To this day, he gets to hear all my dating escapades and juicy stories firsthand.

After chatting and crying a bit, she did the coolest thing. She tucked me in bed like I was a five-year-old on the night before the first day of school. And she prayed with me. Wow! To this day, she is my go-to, number-one fan, and best friend. She and her husband will forever have a huge place in my heart. I wonder if he will read this. **Focus,** Misty.

The next day, I gathered my nerves and headed to my parents' house. The rents! I walked through the door, chit-chatted, and then they asked, "Where's whoochiedoo?" They actually said his name, but this is how we refer to him. Actually, we call him doo snake.

Here is a funny story and another sidebar. When I lived in Los Angeles, my aunt and I used to travel to do stand-up. One early evening, we came back, and my uncle was holding my two-year-old cousin. She was wearing a beautiful dress and pointing to it, saying, "Doo snake, doo doo snake!" My aunt said, "What is she saying?" My uncle said, "Oh there was a snake at the birthday party, and it pooped on her." My aunt said, "One, why did you let her hold a snake and, two, why is she still in that dress?"

A few months later, my aunt, my cousin, and I were in the car on the freeway. The freeway in Los Angeles is ridiculous. You would only need to go two exits, and it would take you forty-five minutes to get there. So this guy cuts off my aunt, and she grabbed the wheel and started shouting, "You, you, mother, you, you, doo snake!" She looked at me, and we both burst out laughing. Oh, my word, that was freaking hilarious; road rage at its finest.

Fast forward a few years. My brother has taught my toddler niece sign language so she can communicate. The entire family is out to eat. My brother is at one end, and me at the other. He was competing with me to tell a story. He snapped his fingers at me and then signs the snake, then the opposite hand going down. So, it looked like a snake pooping. I spit out my drink, and we both started laughing. I knew exactly what he was referring to.

Back to the ex. Sometimes we do the doo snake motions when his name is mentioned. Ok, so it was only like three times. Ish!

And now back to my salvation. Geezalou, Misty! So I'm at my parents' house, and they were asking where he was . . . I said, "He's at home and, by the way, we are getting a divorce!" On like the third night, I was boohooing snot bubble. I do not cry very much, but when I do, man, it is gross.

So, I was crying hysterically in the rocking chair. Remember my brother and I fighting over a dumb chair? **THAT chair!** I fell out of the chair and onto my knees, almost as if I had floated. I bowed my head and said, "Lord, I need you like I've never needed you before. I do not want to live, not like this. The pain, it hurts so much. I cannot live like this anymore. Please come take control. Show me how to live again."

I felt this warm blanket slowly surround and cover me. It was so comforting, this calm, loving presence. I felt God's presence, and it was so beautiful, so needed.

I finally surrendered.

The next morning, I called my ex and said, "You want the divorce, you leave, and I'm going back to the condo!" I felt bolder and a little more confident because I learned to surrender to God, not man.

On a day in March 2019, I had a meltdown, a baby jumbo as my college roommate would call it. I cried in the fetal position for hours listening to worship music. For a few months, God allowed me to test the waters with life and dating yet **again**.

Yes, I am still learning to submit to the Lord, to rest in him. He gave me an image: God is a tree trunk. I was standing on a branch, and he was allowing me to walk away from the trunk to see how far I would go. I would look back to the trunk and say, "Lord I see you; I hear you."

However, I would take another step away. It seemed I was hanging around those not on the same path as me; a drink here and stay out too late there, a date with someone not appropriate for me. Anyway, days after my meltdown, I had a vision of me with my back to the tree trunk, sitting down on the branch, and swinging my legs. Like a little kid with cutoff jeans and a white T-shirt dirtied from playing on the edge, I was finally back with the Lord, and he was supporting my back.

The weekend of the baby jumbo, I felt so much pressure, as in a cocoon, and would feel this dark pressure all around me. While worshiping, I finally laughed and found some relief. Eventually, I felt it break, and it lifted away. I told God, "I feel like I should be a pearl or diamond now, but still I am not."

God is still working on and refining me. I am a pearl and diamond in the making. Life is a journey, not a destination. Enjoy the ride, and stop to smell the roses. To quote Bubba Gump, "life is like a box of chocolates; you never know what is inside." So, why not try a bite of all the chocolates? That is my motto anyway. We can rest when we die. Right? Well, not exactly.

Submission and obedience seem to be my lifelong lesson. The Lord has really been working on me, and I have been thinking a lot about submission and rest. What does it really mean from a biblical standpoint, and why do I have an issue with it? Because when dating, we are supposed to submit to the Lord, not man.

Even though I surrendered parts of my life to the Lord, I still struggled with submission, so much so that the Lord showed me an image: the tail end of a donkey! **Yes**, a donkey. I was being a jack arse with my heels in the ground, and he was trying to pull me into something better, to pull me out of my rut, but I kept resisting. Yes, even though I have surrendered part of my life to the Lord, I still struggle with totally submitting. You feel that you are losing yourself and, in a way, you are; but what is refined through submission is truth!

With guidance, we all need to do what we need to do in this life, gain what we are to have, and meet who we are supposed to meet, allowing ourselves the capacity to become who we are meant to become, and allowing ourselves to grow in the areas we need to grow. Once we can submit, truly surrender, and become obedient, we will finally find that our heels become unstuck from the ground, and we can now follow the Lord on the path he has for us with clarity and ease, which is the way, the truth, and the life.

In Romans 15:4, it reads, "For everything written in the past, was written to teach us, so that through endurance and the encouragement of the scriptures we might have hope." My prayer for you is that God will fill you with all joy and peace as you learn to trust him, believe in Him to guide your life, and you may overflow with that hope filled by the power of the Holy Spirit.

IV

THE "T" IN MISTY

"Never let the fear of striking out get in your way."
– Babe Ruth

TRUST THE PROCESS

We need to learn to hide God's Word around our motives which an be found in our hearts; this is the only thing that transforms our lives. To do this, we need to purge, take inventory of our friends, things, our life, and to get rid of and release what we do not need or from whatever holds us back or tries to keep us down.

Do not rush the process. Let the Lord do what he wants and needs to do in you. Let him peel back the layers one by one, one at a time. If you go too fast, you can potentially become overwhelmed and want to stop; oftentimes walking away from the healing.

Then you are in a rut, stuck, and have to go around the mountain **again** and **again**.

With that said, **do not** wallow in your misfortune or what looks like adversity. Ask God what you need to learn from this and ask him to get you the heck out of dodge. We will experience hardship, sadness, and frustration; it's just a part of life on this side of heaven. Learn from it. Let it help you build character.

The Bible says in Romans 5:3–5 ". . . because we know that suffering produces perseverance, perseverance, character and character hope. And hope does not put us to shame, because God's love has been poured out into our hearts through the Holy Spirit, who was given to us."

Hope!

Hope for the future.

Hope for YOUR future.

Patience is important during the process of allowing God to refine us. I am not saying it is fun or easy, but it is necessary. Over the last few years, people have said I was a wild stallion and needed to quit hanging out with little ponies. The problem with that is I was a wild stallion that needed to be tamed, ok, refined. I asked a friend who has horses, "How do you break a horse?" He said, "You tie them to a post and keep them there until they stop fighting and resisting."

In doing research on taming wild horses, one must first catch the animal. We have to acknowledge there is a God. God tries to reveal himself to us daily; we just miss it because we are running around like chickens with our heads cut off, going to and fro with all the things we think need to be done or are avoiding (i.e., hurt, bills, etc.).

Next, one has to halter the animal, letting God find his way into our hearts has to happen before he can refine us. Then one can start to lead the animal; we start hearing and seeing things God reveals to us, things that need to be addressed so we can move on.

Moving forward can start with grooming the animal, getting closer or more intimate with them. That is God reminding you of who you are.

For me, it was this desire to start dressing classier and wearing more makeup. I actually found some anointing oils that mean different things and started praying those blessings over me, almost like Esther, before she was presented to the king. She had to do six months of beauty treatments, mine has just taken a tad bit longer.

Then one can start handling the animals' hooves. I am not sure if you are ticklish. I am not. But if you are, then this is a little scary, right? Our feet are our foundation, to use a real estate term. We stand on our feet and use our feet to get us from point A to point B. Jesus even washed the disciples' feet as a sign of love and service.

At this point, one can finally tie the animal. Put a harness around it. That is God using the Holy Spirit to woo us, to say it is ok to be where we are, but we don't have to stay that way.

And this is the last step to taming a horse or donkey, which is so appropriate for me. **Flashback**:

Remember when I mentioned God showing me I was being the tail end of a donkey?

Finally, one can get the animal into the trailer to take it for more training or to safety. We finally surrender to God **all** areas within our lives, all hurt, and everything that hinders us from walking into God's best for our lives. This is definitely how God had to tame me, **one** step at a time. And I finally stopped running away, running from God, and running from my past.

After this wonderful revelation, my dear friend Donna sent me a text: SMALL STRAWS IN A SOFT WIND by *Marsha Burns* this was on August 3, 2020: I speak to those who feel like a racehorse waiting for the gate to open. You're prancing up and down will not make the gate open any quicker. Settle down. Conserve your strength and energy. The time will come when you can run the race again, and you will run well. Now is not that time. Be patient. *Luke 21:19 "By your patience possess your souls."*

While 2020 was hard for almost everyone on the entire planet, it gave me time I had not previously taken for the last piece of my transformation that needed to happen. I slowed down, mostly because the entire world did. I started going for walks in the mornings as well as most evenings. This was my time with the Lord. I got to see the sun set, hear the beautiful birds chirping, wave to all my neighbors, and listen to the audible Bible. I have never done that before. It was good to hear it and let it pierce my heart and soul.

As I got into the Word, I would read scripture and was like, "What does that Word really mean?" It also made me reflect on things I wanted and things I did not want in a companion, my business, and my health.

In my twenties, I made a list of qualities I wanted in a mate. I think there were about thirty things on the original list. I hid the list in a journal, and one day, someone was like, "Oh, you need to tear up that list and just know God knows what you need." I burned the letter. I also burned everything I had from my ex-husband. It's very cleansing and therapeutic.

Years later, I heard a pastor say, "You need to be specific when you ask the Lord for things." So, guess what, I started a **new** list. It was probably not exactly as my original list, but I am more mature now! Right. And then I made a list of qualities that I felt were **my** best qualities and what I felt I had to offer. Well, my list wasn't as long as the qualities of a mate that I expected him to have. I went back to **his** list and put the fruit of the Spirit by the ones that really mattered; love, joy, peace, patience, kindness, faithfulness, goodness, gentleness, and self-control. Ok, so nice fingernails, big calves, and pouty lips are still on my list, since "you have not because you ask not." So if it is in the Bible, and I believe the Bible is true, then why can't I ask for those things and God bless my request?

After going back in my journal, I also found that during this process, I had made a list of the lessons

I had learned and wanted to bring into my next marriage. Some of those things are:

- Be an obedient wife (this was even before my *submission* guy);
- Keep a clean organized house;
- Not to compete with my spouse (I do not mean like playing board games, etc.);
- Lift up my husband with kind and encouraging words (I do that with other people; why did not I do that before?);
- Communicate with my spouse and let him into my heart (I was not able to with my ex as I had not even allowed the Lord into my heart. Wow!);
- Do things I want done (I always wanted a romantic picnic. I told him I wanted this, and he never did it. So, the point is I should have planned and implemented it instead of waiting for him to do it);
- I do not need to be in control (this has been years in the making); and

- I am not as strong as I think I am (another ouch).

Sheila Walsh says in her book, *The Longing in Me,* that if we choose to live a vulnerable, transparent life, we invite that in others too. When we are molested, abused, beaten, or betrayed, trust is broken, and we can find it hard to distinguish the difference between love and sex. When we are not healed from our past, we can bring that fear, anger, disappointment, and rejection into our present and potentially our future, whether we mean to or not. It creeps back in through a harsh word or inappropriate touch, often triggering a negative response that reminds us of the past. You either react negatively or push those closest to you away.

In my case, I used sex as a weapon, which resulted in pushing away the very one I should have let in the closest. One of the reasons I did this was I had an issue with confrontation. I have to admit something, confrontation makes me physically sick to my stomach. Now I know people that say, "I do not like confrontation," yet they are the ones causing it, or say "I hate drama," but they stir the drama up.

I had to deal with some things I had put aside that I was hoping would magically go away' which never do, by the way. Don't be like me and wait years to confront something that will set you free if you would just deal with it. I kept asking God why certain things had to happen in my life. Why did this happen to me, and why did they do that to me? I couldn't move on because I kept focusing on the **why**.

I shared with a friend some of the things going on in my life, and she said, "Let go of the **why** and focus on the **who**. Let go of what others have done unto you so that you can do unto others." She shared Scripture that had been on her mind for a week, and realized it was for me.

Progress isn't always visible. So, stay the course to healing, purging, refining, and becoming the best version of yourself. As Rocky Balboa says, "It ain't about how hard you're hit. It's about how hard you can get hit and keep moving forward."

I also love this from Sheila's book: "Let your identity come from the way God rescued you and not with what you needed rescuing from." Not everyone needs to know every detail of your story, but your story definitely could help someone who is stuck exactly where you are right now.

Trust God during this process, or let him start the process. Don't let the things of this world be more important than crossing over! Don't let the fear of striking out keep you from crossing over into what God has for you.

Before I forget, through all of what I've shared with you, there is a main ingredient required to implement along with trusting the process: rest! Yes, that word again. I say we can rest when we die. But God rested on the seventh day, and it was good. If you are a type-A personality, a firstborn, or a high-strung individual like me, then you know we tend to run the candle at both ends—juggle jobs, family, church, dating, and whatever else everyone needs. I'm a fixer, problem-solver, and make-stuff-happen kinda gal. It's hard for us to slow down. At least it is for me.

Early last year, I was at a friend's house watching a seminar. The seminar would stop, and the facilitator would call for dance breaks. My friend and I started jumping up and down to the music. I landed, and **boom**, I felt my calf snap. I immediately bent over, grabbed my calf, and started praying. I limped to the couch, where I remained until it was time to leave. I limped to my car, where I called my sister-in-law (SIL), who is a doctor. For the next couple of weeks (it felt like months), I wore a boot and had to slow down.

When I walked my normal stride, it hurt, but when I took baby steps, it didn't hurt. Aha! The Lord showed me that when we take too big a step, we pull things out of alignment. My calf was only pulled; thankfully, it did not rip apart. But I had to take smaller steps so it would not hurt.

Slowing down AKA rest allows our bodies to heal, our minds to clear, and our hearts to mend. Jesus told the disciples, "Come to me, ALL who are weary and carry heavy burdens, and I will give you rest." The Message Translation says, ". . . get away with me and you'll recover your life." Only when we come to Jesus, truly lay our burdens down, and cast our cares to Him will we get rest, and our lives will recover.

God promises great blessings to his people, but many of these blessings take active participation. He will deliver us from fear, save us out of our troubles, guard and deliver us, show us goodness, supply our needs, listen when we talk to him, and redeem us, but we must do our part. We can appropriate his blessings when we seek him, cry out to him, trust him, fear him, refrain from lying, turn from evil, do good and seek peace, are humble, and serve him.

You've heard the scripture, "Taste and see that the Lord is good." "Taste and see" does not mean

"Check out what God can do for you." Instead, it's a warm invitation. Try this. I know you'll like it!

When we take the first step of obedience in following God, we will discover that he is good and kind. When we begin the Christian life, our knowledge of God is partial and incomplete. As we trust him daily, we experience how good he is.

"Fear the Lord" means to show deep respect and honor to him. We demonstrate true reverence by our humble attitude and genuine worship. Which leads to surrendering or submission.

Many may question David's advice in Psalm 34:8 because we seem to lack numerous good things. This is not a blanket promise that Christians will have everything they want. Instead, this is David's praise for God's goodness—all those who call upon God in their need will be answered, sometimes in unexpected ways.

Remember, God knows what we need; our deepest needs are spiritual. Even though many Christians face unbearable poverty and hardship, they still have enough spiritual nourishment to live for God. David said that to have God is to have all you really need. God is enough. God is more than enough. If you don't have everything you need, ask:

I.   Is this really a need;

II. Is this really good for me; and

III. Is this the best time for me to have what I desire?

Even if you answer **yes** to all three questions, God may allow you to go without to help you grow more dependent on Him. He may want you to learn that you need him more than having to achieve your immediate desires.

Sarah McLachlan is a musician who writes love ballads. One day after hearing her song, "Ice Cream," this is what God revealed in lyric conversation:

Your love is better than ice cream, better than anything else I've tried, and your love is better than ice cream, everyone here knows how to fight . . .

God's love is better than ice cream. We lose control over our emotions, but God handles it for us, so we don't have to fight our battles alone.

And it's a long way down, it's a long way down to the place where we started from.

When we are hurt, we usually shut out God's love. We isolate ourselves, which can lead to depression.

Your love is better than chocolate, better than anything else I've tried. Oh, love is better than chocolate, everyone here knows how to cry.

God's love is better than chocolate; everyone has something that has made us cry. You can't eat chocolate or ice cream and be mad. Can you? So, surrender your heart to our Lord today so you can taste and see that the Lord is good.

V

THE "Y" IN MISTY

"Only those who will risk going too far can possibly find out how far one can go."

– T. S. Elliot

YIELDING OUT OF THE WILDERNESS

Lord, I'm sick of going around the mountain. I'm ready to walk in the land of milk and honey. Just like the Israelites went around the mountain for forty years, I feel like I have been going around this mountain **for e v e r**, and it's time for a different path.

David hid in a cave for thirteen years as an outcast with no home. He constantly watched his back because he didn't know when or if his enemy would catch up with him. Those years in darkness, a lonely place on a foreign land, had only deepened his relationship with God and finely tuned his heart and ears to God's voice. Instead of asking God to help or rescue him, he finally asked God what to do!

Here I am, thirteen years after a divorce. I may not be an outcast, but as a single, I have felt that way plenty of times. Most classes and events at churches are about families or couples. Most of my friends are married, so hanging out with them feels like the third or, sometimes, fifth wheel.

I constantly allowed the enemy to tell me, "You are not going to find someone. You are not really over your pain; you let everyone think you are this fun, happy-go-lucky person. You are a fake, a phony!" However, just like David, these last thirteen years of darkness, my lonely foreign place, I have learned to tune my heart and ear to listen to God's voice and remember his promises to me, promises that I would meet someone! For God said, "It is not good for man to be alone."

Here we are in the middle of a pandemic, with so much uncertainty, doubt, fear. But for me, it has been amazing! My mornings have become routine:

wake up, walk Lady, then sit in my mint green, velvet, Victorian chair with my feet up on my bed and read the Word of God; Asking him what to do! He sent me to Deuteronomy 17:14, where it says, "you are about to enter the land the Lord is giving you."

Oh boy, this is exciting. I am learning to decrease my flesh so He can increase in my life. I think before I open my mouth. I am not quick to offer suggestions to fix other people's problems. Sometimes they just need to hear themselves talk it out. Oh wait, that's how I figure things out for myself. I finally said to the Lord, "I give you my heart when it comes to men. You know better what I need than I do." And I asked Him to remove unrealistic expectations.

For so long, I had lived in this fantasy world I called the Mystique Land of Misty, where everything was purple, sparkly, everyone would laugh and be kind, and I was in control of, well, **everything**. Thankfully, I am finally seeing that God never leaves us broken and He was making me whole. We don't have to live in fantasy land to hide from the hurt when we let Him do it, layer by layer.

I had quite a few layers; I mean, it has taken thirteen years. I have allowed the Lord to help me get over being independent and headstrong. My mom once told me she raised me to be independent, but I was **too** independent. God showed me I was when I finally sat down to **listen** to what he still needed to do in me to stop going around the mountain and learn to be dependent on him; he would provide all my needs and fulfill all my desires. All the things we look to a husband for, God was the only one that could actually do those things.

A friend introduced me to The Passion Translation of the Bible. Y'all, 1 Corinthians 13:4–8 literally **wrecked** me. It's long, so be patient. *WINK WINK*

Love is large and incredibly patient. Love is gentle, and consistently kind to all. It refuses to be jealous when blessing comes to someone else. Love does not brag about one's own achievements nor inflate its own importance. Love does not traffic in shame and disrespect, nor selfishly seek its own honor. Love is not easily irritated or quick to take offense. Love celebrates honesty and finds no delight in what is wrong. Love is a safe place of shelter, for it never stops believing the best for others. Love never takes failure as defeat, for it never gives up. Love never stops loving!

After reading it out loud, I felt such peace and freedom to know God's love, which is perfect and perfects me every day.

"Love is a safe place of shelter" brought me to my knees. I had never thought of God's love that way before. He never stops loving us.

Then this thought came over me: Christ died for all of us, even those that would never receive Him! Wow! So, that puts a new twist on loving your enemies, right? I had already forgiven those that hurt me. It was not until I read this verse that I truly had compassion for all of them. They, too, were hurting, and you know the saying that we hurt the ones closest to us, or hurting people hurt people. Allow God's love to wash over you and heal every raw spot in your heart!

Later in 2020, one of my spiritual moms had a word for me that God had impressed upon her:

God says you are a RUNNER. God says I will place you in the right place at the right time, but you must always remember that the fastest runner does not always win the race, and the strongest does not always win the battle. Be careful to be disciplined, patient, and endurance is the key to winning the race. You must be quick to lay aside every weight or sin that would easily beset you. If you will run with me, I will summon, as I have said before, a runner that will run with you in due time.

I dove into these words and meditated on them. Discipline is the practice of training people to obey rules or a code of behavior, activity, or experience that provides mental or physical training, the discipline for me was making time for the Lord.

Patience is needed with this journey and looking forward to what and who God has for me. And endurance is needed to run the race God has called me to. Now with total transparency, I have good days and not-so-good days. If it is cloudy too many days in a row, it affects me and my mood.

I have shared a bunch of my not-so-good days, so I want to share a good day. I have a favorite movie, *Under the Tuscan Sun* with Diane Lane. She gets divorced, goes on vacation to Italy, and purchases a bungalow that needs rehabbing. It takes her some time to get over the divorce and to start enjoy life. She's in Tuscany, her neighbor owns a vineyard, and life could not be better, right?

In one scene, she meets a guy, Marcello. Ok, he is more than a guy; he's handsome and romantic. She spends this amazing weekend with him doing things I said I wouldn't do until my wedding night. So, when she gets home, she realizes she's not depressed anymore, then she actually smiles and realizes she actually wants to smile. So, she jumps on her bed, grabs her breasts, and says, "I knew it. I knew it!" She finally let go of the hurt and embraced a moment that brought her joy and a lot of satisfaction.

My point is this, one day you will wake up and have a thought, "Hey, I am happy, I am truly happy. I am no longer wearing the badge of fear, anxiety, or sadness of the past." You are free to be the best version of yourself and be in the perfect position to receive God's best for your life.

In Mark 4, Jesus told a story of a farmer that sowed seed in his land. Some seed fell on a path, some on a rocky path, some around thorns, and some on good soil. The seed that fell on the path was eaten by birds. The seed that fell on the rocky place was scorched by the sun because it did not have deep roots, and the ones that fell on the thorny area were choked by the plant, so it didn't bear fruit. The seed that was planted on good and fertile soil produced a crop, some thirty, some sixty, and some one hundred times what was sown. Jesus told the disciples that the seed on the path was like Satan coming and taking away the Word that was sown in them.

In my story, I prayed God would bring me someone to love, but I allowed that person or relationship to stop or hinder my relationship with the Lord because I had stopped praying.

Going to church became a fight. Would he go with me, or be mad because I went without him, or would I be mad all day because I didn't go? Eventually, I did not go at all because I was tired of the Sunday morning fights. The seed that fell on the rocky place Jesus explained was not rooted, so it only lasted a short time.

You don't have a lot in common, but he is so attractive. Remember, he did not want to get married again, have more kids, and was atheist. I had to cut that off immediately because it would not have lasted anyway. It would have been fun for a while, but we would not have made roots together.

Sidebar:

Undiscouraged and undefeated, Paul wrote powerful letters of encouragement from prison. Paul did not ask the Ephesians to pray that his chains would be removed but that he would continue to speak fearlessly for Christ despite them.

God can use us in any circumstance to do His will. Even as we pray for a change in our circumstances, we should also pray that God will accomplish His plan through us right where we are.

Regarding the seed that fell on the thorns, Jesus said the worries of life, deceitfulness of wealth, and desires of other things choked out the plant and were unfruitful. Had I continued on course with the turkey, he would have choked out my personality; my joy and I would have ended up browbeaten and stuck at home dealing with life by myself while he was out thinking he was saving the world.

On the seed that fell on good soil, you hear the Word, accept it, and it produces a crop some thirty times, some sixty, and some one hundred times what was sown. You meet someone, and you get what you put in, right? If you give someone 30 percent of effort, you get 30 percent in return, and so on. Do you want to give 100 percent to the right one, one that will yield a 100 percent fruitful crop?

Stability comes from deep roots in the kingdom and system of God. You can only get deep roots by spending time with the Lord, in His Word, and walking in what you have been called to do. One day of yielding to the favor of God is better than a generation of labor. I do not know about you, but I want to yield a crop that is 100 percent fruitful, fully rooted in love, joy, peace, patience, kindness, goodness, faithfulness, gentleness, and self-control. I only want God's best! So, Lord, I give you 100 percent!

They say you meet someone when you least expect it. One night, I was at dinner with a friend at my favorite restaurant. After dinner, he said, "Do you want me to walk you to your car?" I said, "No, I'm going to hang out with the owner at the bar, but thank you." The owner saw me and said, "Hey Misty, come over here; we are doing a wine tasting tonight, and I've already poured you a glass." I visited with some others at the bar for a bit and said to the bartender, "Hey Stella, I need to go to the ladies' room; will you watch my stuff?"

As I walked back from the bathroom, there was this handsome gentleman staring at me at the end of the bar. I looked away and then looked back, and he was still staring at me. I smiled, and he smiled back. As I walked past him, I saw he was eating my favorite dish there and said, "Are you enjoying the pasta?" He said, "It's my favorite meal here."

"Me too."

"This is my favorite restaurant."

"Me too."

"I come here all the time."

"Me too . . ."

TO BE CONTINUED . . .

HOPE RISING CHALLENGE

Thank you for allowing me to share my story. I hope you found some faith, hope, and healing along the way. I would like to encourage you, no, challenge you to:

- Journal daily: seeing our thoughts on paper allows us to recognize patterns and can hopefully reveal areas you can let God work on;

- Make a bucket list: share your list and start experiencing them with others;

- Surround yourself with awesome people: and remove those who are not awesome.

Sometimes it's just for a season; however, sometimes you must live life without them;

- Serve and volunteer: find something to do beyond yourself. It's hard to wallow in your misery when you are doing for others; and
- Take care of yourself: mind, body, spirit, health, and things that bring you joy.

Life is too short, and there is so much fun to be had. So, stop to smell the roses, paint that picture, save for that crazy awesome vacation, write a book, go skydiving, and learn a new language.

Keep in mind, some of the things are on my list for a couple years before I am able to do them. But make a plan and get a friend on board so you'll stick with it!

ACKNOWLEDGEMENTS

I have many thank yous because I have many awesome people in my life.

First, I want to thank my amazing parents for always supporting me, no matter what. You have always been my number-one fans—during the Texas humidity of summer track to long weekends at volleyball tourneys, basketball, and cross-country meets; for believing in me when I didn't believe in myself. I admire your dedication to our family. Y'all got married young; thank you for sticking it out, now get to enjoying retirement! I'm honored to be your oldest and test run, *wink wink*. Mom, you are my reality check, whose soothing voice I need to hear when I don't feel good. Dad, you are my ego boost, I appreciate your infectious enthusiasm. Thanks for always pushing me.

To T.C. III, our main man, top cat and accident pro. You are my favorite brother, OK you are my only brother. I admire you, am honored to call you my best friend and love talking to you almost every day where we solve world and family problems that no one asked our opinion for. I love you more more!

To *Donna,* my first spiritual mom and now my best friend. Thank you for listening to all my crazy stories, checking in on me when you haven't heard from me in a while, telling me the hard stuff, and interpreting all my dreams. I admire and love you beyond words. Who knew a job would lead to such a beautiful friendship? But God . . .

To *Deen,* my second spiritual mom, whose guidance has been instrumental in my painful growth walk with the Lord. You also are not afraid to tell me the hard stuff. And I am eternally grateful for your obedience and admire your dedication to teaching women how to have a deep relationship with the Lord and encouraging us to walk in our giftings. *Billie* my third spiritual mom, whose dedication to the Lord is admired by so many. I am also thankful for your words of encouragement . . .

To *Donna, Deen, Billie, Jacque, Bill, Pastor Greg,* and those no longer with us: *John, Dorcia,* and *Darlene,* my spiritual family and mentors in the faith. I am who I am today because of your obedience to the Lord, dedication to walking out your spiritual gifts, and never wavering faith. It has truly been a blessing and honor to have you in my life. I pray I am able to keep putting into action what I have learned from each of you.

To Tracy & Stacey my CS3, I love getting together for Bible study, sharing life with you lovely ladies is such a blessing deep in my soul.

To *Melissa* for being my awesome unicorn bestie, and always encouraging me to stay weird. To *Brittany* for sharing your single experience and encouraging me that others needed to hear my story.

ABOUT THE AUTHOR

I am a true blond with blue eyes, five-foot-seven, and weigh, well, that is to be determined. I have struggled with my weight after several surgeries for endometriosis, most recently losing twenty-one pounds; however, I still have quite a few to go.

I grew up in a small town between Houston and Galveston. I hate wearing watches and forget to wear earrings quite often. I love to laugh and more superlatively to make others laugh.

My laugh is pretty loud and possibly obnoxious. I am aware of this and sometimes snort, catching myself from laughing too loudly.

I'm the oldest child with a younger brother whom I talk to several times a week, often multiple times a day. We are working on purchasing our first house to flip. And I am a real estate broker, owning my brokerage.

I was a mother of two fur babies; however, both of them are no longer with me. One day, I hope to adopt more pups, but I do not miss being slobbered on or waking up with a paw in my face or ear. However, I do miss their sweet kisses and barking conversations with me.

In my twenties, I did standup comedy in New York, Los Angeles, and Houston.

I am in several Bible study groups and enjoy painting, photography, fine dining, reading, organizing fun for friends and family, and fake baking. These are only a few of my pastimes. In my downtime, I serve on several real estate community committees and have served as a CASA, a court appointed special advocate for children in CPS cases.

I have a heart to help the homeless, the fatherless and widows.